AF483643

DRACO ALCHEMICUS

A love story

Draco Alchemicus

ACT I: THE CASINO

by
Dragon Common Room

Kimberly Crilly
Jacqueline Khalfan
Ken Ramsey
Mel Wiggin

Illustrations by
Zé Nuno Fraga

Edited by
Rachel Fulton Brown

DCR

Draco Alchemicus
Act I: The Casino

Published by DCR Books.

979-8-218-25696-8 Print
979-8-218-25698-2 Ebook

And as Moses lifted up the serpent in the desert, so must the
Son of man be lifted up: That whosoever believeth in him
may not perish, but may have life everlasting.

John 3:14–15

Prologue

In rainbow time, when dragons hoarded gold
and pirates sailed the seas in search of spice,
a city shimmered with electric cold,
its storerooms stocked with precious merchandise,
where dreams were bought and sold at dealers' price.
A court convened, ruled by a sovereign snake
whose virtue was to capture slaves with vice.
No spells could bind the alchemical Drake,
until one day a stranger came, its spells to break.

He raids the City at the gate of night,
a humble pigeon nestled at his breast,
for he has come to play the game of light
against the darkness of the Dragon's breath
and win his love back from the jaws of death.
A faerie Queen has seized the merchants' trove
and calls herself by name Elizabeth.
The pirate King comes forth with hound and dove;
he goes to war to slay the snake and claim his love.

Act I: The Casino

1

A band of crystal lit with heaven's fire
burst o'er the earth and flashed across the plain,
reverberating through the raining pyre
of stories sung in cities built by Cain.
A pinioned cloud danced rings around the flame,
its cooing harmonized with chords of grace.
A deep base note encoded love reclaimed
from kingdom's fall of mankind's ancient race.
The resonating wings revealed a clouded face.

2

The pigeon aether undulated free,
an orchestra of feathers white as frost.
The wingéd loom descended on the sea;
from light it spun a subatomic cross.
Bright feathers knit atomic Helios,
while oscillating sparks set fire to quills.
Reverberating wings turned light to dust.
The looming man from loom that seemed to trill
emerged in flesh from cloud of sapphire-blue beryl.

3

The chorus swelled; the man stepped onto land,
from clouds delivered to the darkened shore.
He stood there naked, looking at the sand;
his face shone bright like heated iron ore.
White strands of hair presaged the coming war,
while from his lips came songs in ancient tongue
not heard since towers fell to angels' lore.
He took a breath like snakes soak up the sun;
his voice like thunder rolling o'r the waves, he sung:

4

"I loved you from the first glance of your eye;
your garden was a paradise of doves.
I came into my kingdom from the sky
because you left me languishing with love.
I called you to my wrist, my falcon's glove,
and promised I would warm you at my breast
with aromatic spices from above.
The winter now has gone, the rain has passed;
arise, make haste, my love, my dove, my one most blessed."

5

A single tear ran down his bearded cheek
as, longing, he looked toward the City's spires.
A bird was gliding on a thermal peak
in search of mankind's live electric wires,
the currency with which to win empires.
The man raised up his arm with outstretched wrist
to welcome pigeon to his heart's desires,
and when the dove perched there, just like a kiss,
it promised such a love that brings eternal bliss.

6

The man beheld the City's grand arcade,
a castle rising from a quartzite sea.
Its jeweléd towers glittered in array;
bright diadems of gem machinery
banked currents of the great electron sea.
Glass arches framed a crystalline flambeau
where golden walls reflected fractured beams.
As water burns with luminescent glow,
he walked unshod along the bright electric bow.

7

His feet left prints of blue along the strand,
the waters phosphorescing with the tide,
while from the City came the sound of hands
all clapping to one rhythm like a hive.
The music of the bees called him to dive
into the frenzied humming at its core,
a hypnotech of elemental jive.
Its sweetness called his heart unbound to soar;
the scent of honey left him hungering for more.

8

A growl behind him made him turn his head.
A wild dog stood his ground, a canine guard.
"I have no food for you," the traveler said,
and to the hound he gave no more regard.
He stepped with doom upon the boulevard
that wound its way up to the City Gate.
The paving stones in serpentine were hard;
beneath his feet, they seemed to know their fate.
The Canaan dog ran at his heels, his thirst to sate.

9

The man was naked, no clothes for his loins.
Upon the stones, he found discarded skins
that shimmered in the twilight vespertine
like gemstones washed in rivers before sin.
Around his waist, tied with an armored pin
he wrapped the scales the boa left behind,
silks patched in colors like the Harlequin.
Its texture hymned its ancient crawl through time.
"Who goes there?" cried a voice like God's own seraphim.

10

"I am the man who's running out of time,
the warper and the weaver of the web.
I come to claim my bride, fair Columbine,
whose journey I have followed from the crib."
The guard regarded him with mirth, and said:
"You seek love here? A drug for fools! I'd wage
you'll kill yourself upon a lonely bed.
A liquor would be easier to gauge;
those who love start wild, then they fly into a cage."

11

"It is for this that I have come to town—
to gamble that my bride remembers me."
"It's your funeral, mate," the bouncer frowned;
he gestured towards the house magneto-screen.
A metal arch stood flashing tourmaline
to scan the people as they came to play.
The man stepped 'cross the lintel regally
into a grand illumined hall of games.
Six chandeliers shone their lights on the night's ballet.

12

He stood beneath a dome of tow'ring height.
The ceiling of the room was far away;
a false sky met his gaze with twinkling lights,
a belt of time in Zodiac array.
Gold curtains fell like waterfalls, risqué
and riverine they flowed around the vault.
The veils were drawn across the grand archways
and framed the ceiling made of dark cobalt.
The neon lights flashed on and off like flaming salt.

13

A sea of bronze upheld by oxen pairs
stood brimful with the waters of the skies.
The waters poured out over stony stairs
into a fountain filled with golden bribes.
A sterling current rolled its liquid ice
spewed by a dragon from the fountain's hearth,
while on its base were words deeply incised:
"All fate's a wager—boldly now cast forth!
Dame Fortune favors those who go in quest of worth."

14

Four faces ringed the watery wheel of chance:
a man, a bull, a lion, and a drake.
Laid out in gemstones on the floor, they danced,
and bowed down towards the brazen oxen lake.
Their wings were dazzling in the water's wake;
four bodies were of men, three faces beasts.
The creatures proffered; who would treasure take?
The man surveyed them, north, south, west, and east.
Their mouths gaped open, hungering for souls to feast.

15

"It's pretty trippy, yes?" a woman said.
"Buy me a drink? You look like you've got style."
She pursed her lips—her mouth blood-diamond red—
then gently tossed her hair to make him smile.
"Why linger wasting time on this sundial?
I know some games that could keep us amused.
Here, come with me," she gestured to the aisle.
Then she looked down, as if somewhat confused.
"Is that your mutt? The management won't be enthused."

16

"The creature's mine," the man replied. "And you?"
"I roll my own dice, don't you fear," she bluffed.
"The chef's to die for here—he's cordon bleu."
"I love a good steak, cooked on flames," he chuffed,
while glancing at the diamonds on her cuffs.
"I was a star once, I can show you things;
in vain some claim this City's not enough!
Men chase fool's gold, but here you don't need wings.
A lucky star like me can make slaves into kings."

17

"I've used a star as guide upon a time.
I wonder where your star will guide me now?"
"It's in the cards! Can you count up to nine?
Or throw the bones, 'cause they're a real cash cow!
Roulette is fun if you like to play foul,
but I would recommend a game of pool.
If you feel lucky, you could try Pai Gow.
For bankers' games, you need to know the rules.
Or stake the one-armed bandit, and collect three jewels."

18

He looked at her; she smiled at him again.
Her hair was shining in the dancing light;
her dress was made of silver, gold, and gems;
a red-tipped ivory cigarette glowed bright.
She winked at him through lashes dark as night,
then blew soft rings of perfume in the air.
Her cheeks were flushed, her teeth were snowy white.
She tilted her head left and asked him fair,
"So, will you join me in the court? I'll lead you there."

19

On diamonds, black and white, she crossed the floor;
her hips swayed with the rhythm of her spine.
Her gold and silver gown, Christian couture,
made promises to all who caught her eye.
As queen of hearts, she numbered her demense,
while players paused their games at twenty-one.
Bedazzled by the glory of their queen,
they counted on her to increase their fun
with cards and every game they played under the sun.

20

"Is Beth your dame?" the bouncer asked the man;
"she comes here, like a muse, to roll the dice."
The man looked up and pointed to the span
of stars that gleamed above their heads like ice.
"You see that dragon there, up in the heights?
Lo! I remember it as but a viper."
"She'll let you play, but calculate her price;
some men forget they've got to pay the piper."
The dog sniffed 'round the lady, hunting for a cipher.

21

One couple caught the man's eye in the hall.
They sat together over tinkling drinks
and holding hands with golden rings, enthralled.
"I like this horse, don't you? What do you think?,"
the newlywed inquired with a wink.
She leaned in close to listen to her man.
"The odds are low," he fiddled with his drink
and looked up from the diamond on her hand.
"These horses might be nags; we need to craft a plan."

22

He pondered riders' weights and saddle lead
and scribbled race notes on his serviette
to verify the blood of thoroughbreds.
His wife picked out her colts by epithet.
"Look! Here's the horse on which we ought to bet!
She's called Andromeda, just like my mom.
The silks are black and red like in roulette.
Her jockey's cute—I saw him in the prom.
The name is key. Her owner's name is Oberon!"

23

"I never asked your name," the lady purred.
She ran soft fingers down his silk-draped arm.
"My name is Drake, Eliza Drake—what's yours?"
"They call me Mr. Stone where I come from."
"That's far too formal! You must have a nom!"
She moved in close, her eyes fixed on his face.
"I'm Damian," he said, eyes hard and strong.
He looked into her heart and found the ace:
this queen of hearts feared love; she feared an amesace.

24

Eliza looked away and scanned the room;
her gaze fell on the couple making bets.
"Those two look like they're on their honeymoon.
Let's toast the lovebirds on their sweet duet!"
She made a beeline straight for their banquette.
The husband put away his racing form
just as the lady burst their tête-à-tête:
"I'm good at numbers—mine always perform.
A shame it is when treasure chests are overdrawn."

25

"Our bets are good," the husband told his wife.
She turned to him with love bright in her eyes.
"Our horse is sure to win—I'd bet my life!"
He looked at her and smiled, "And so would I."
"To go all in the first time isn't wise,"
Eliza gestured towards the starting gate—
"You need to play the track to get the prize.
You wouldn't want to miss out on the plate.
A horse you choose today could be a horse too late."

26

"They're at the gate!" The couple turned to cheer.
The horses lined up, eager for the chase.
The jockeys in their silks were cavalier
about the danger of their blazing pace.
The commentators called out, "Start the race!"
The gates cracked and released the cavalry.
"They're off!" the wife sang, rapture on her face.
She held her hands together, prayerfully;
the thundering of hooves beat out a rhapsody.

27

The fillies flashed across the megascreen,
competing in the pack to make their break.
Each furlong brought them closer to the lead;
each stride they took completely changed the stakes.
The talking heads remarked the give-and-take,
while punters watched Andromeda take third:
"She's running for her life right down the straight!"
The jockey shouted a commanding word;
the filly's pounding heart propelled her past the herd.

28

"That filly was too easy to command,"
Eliza turned to Damian with a grin.
"He rode her hard, just like a little man.
No horse should need a crop to make her win."
She ran a hand along her silk-draped skin.
"I thought she ran with heart," the other speared.
She winced. "This kind of race is new for them,
and like that horse they'll learn the scent of fear."
"And yet the brave run bold into love's wild frontier."

$m\,r\left(\dfrac{2\pi}{T}\right)^2 = G\,\dfrac{m\,M}{r^2} \rightarrow T^2 = \left(\dfrac{4\pi^2}{G\,M}\right)r^2 \rightarrow T^2 \propto r^3$
$m\,r\,\omega^2 = G\,\dfrac{m\,M}{r^2}$

29

"Look, love!" the wife exclaimed. "Our filly won!
Let's celebrate tonight and make a babe!"
The husband grinned and reached for her in fun.
"Perhaps we should consult the astrolabe?"
He wrapped his arm around her slender shape.
The glamorous Ms. Drake flicked back her hair.
"I'd want more dough before I would undrape.
You'd risk a child, so race again—I dare!
So many needs arise for mothers unaware."

30

The wife's smile vanished at her silver tongue.
The husband turned away and clenched his jaw:
"Perhaps we'd better bet another one."
"And when you're stuffed, you don't get to withdraw;
that pleasure's rare when you go full bourgeois.
Just think about the interest you would have
if only progeny you would forestall.
When milk arrives you won't be making half;
the golden cow gets cheaper once she's had her calf."

31

She slid into the booth and crossed her legs.
The wife was tugging at her wedding ring:
"You said you knew the way to vest our egg."
Eliza mused. "I think I've got the thing.
You want to win big in the sport of kings,
but kings aren't crowned until they pay their dues.
To beat the horses, you must test your wings.
Perhaps you'd like to try my liquid Muse?"
And from her breast she took a flask of strange chartreuse.

32

"I've got a drop of something here. It stings,
but when it hits you with its lucid fire,
your eyes will open, and you'll see like kings."
The woman's eyes ignited with desire.
"Who knows what royal riches we'll acquire?!"
She stretched her hand out for the lady's glass
and held it for her husband to admire.
"A toast! To us! to leave the teeming mass!
One draught, and we will soar into the ruling class!"

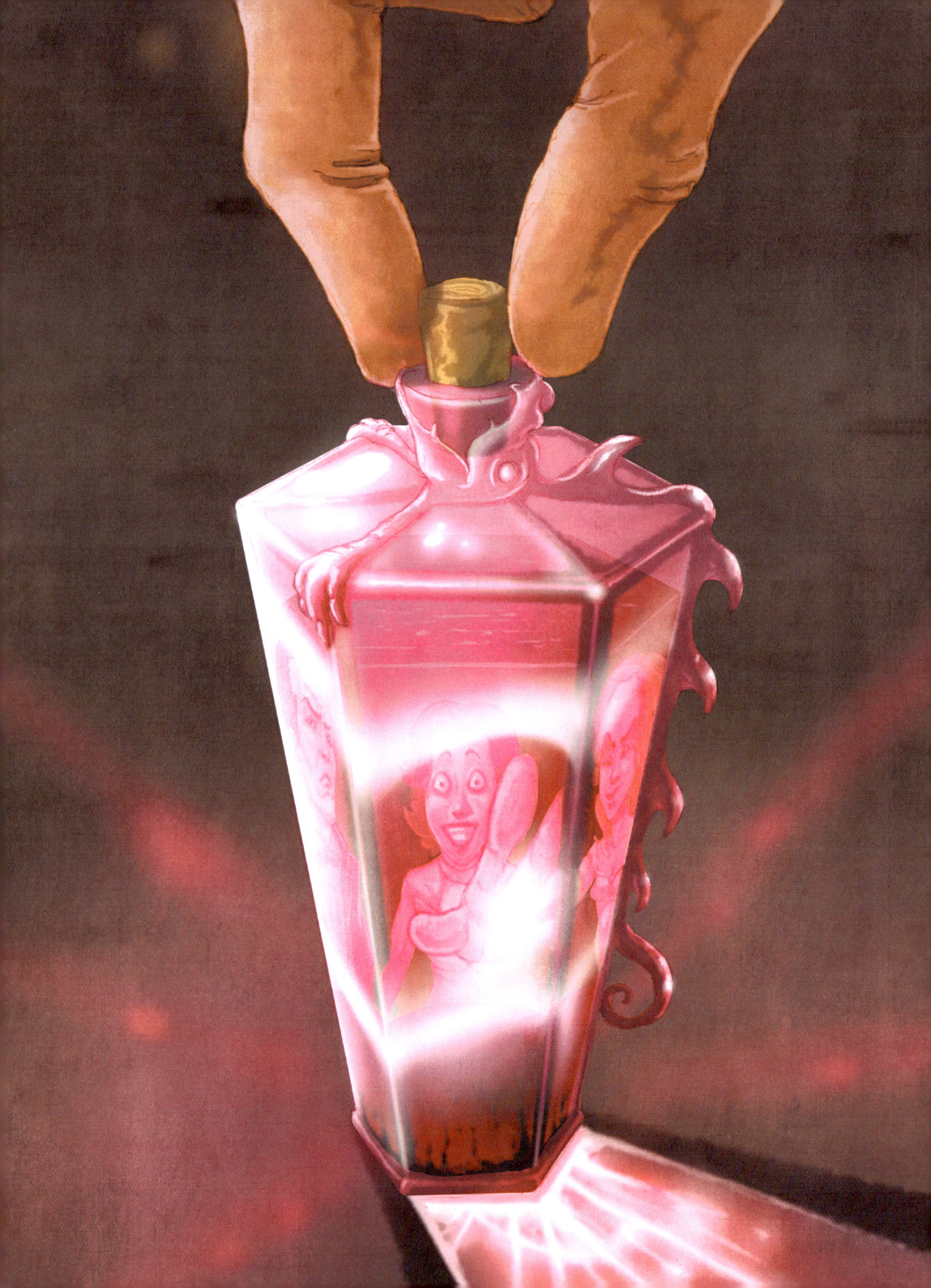

33

A bark from 'neath the table startled her.
"I didn't know they let dogs in the house."
The hound snarled at the vial and raised his fur.
Her husband drew a circle with a cross.
"It's just as good to get a coin to toss!"
"This drink is good to taste," his wife replied.
Eliza handed her another drop.
"What harm's a small sip if it wins the prize?"
The man raised to his lips the drink, sipped once, and sighed.

34

He marked their pick and gestured to his bride.
"How do you feel about this cavalry?"
She said, "I'll use your stats to find our pride,"
then seized his charts to study greedily.
"The risk is high, we could lose mightily."
"This horse could be a winner—Perseus."
"It doesn't feel right—wrong astronomy."
"You'd wager ponies against Morpheus?!"
He gnawed his pencil while his bride tried calculus.

35

"You'll miss the trip. Look now! They're at the gate."
The couple turned their heads in startled awe
to see their stud already in the eight.
His horseshoes cut the turf like iron claws;
he crushed the iron bit between his jaws.
The jockey lashed his crop like lightning strikes
and struck at Perseus, goading him to war.
His gaskins churned their way along the pike,
while voices in the aether screamed into the mic:

36

"It's Clipper Ship, with IrishBreakfastTea!
They're out in front of champion China White.
Now Dynamo is passing Wounded Knee,
and Cannonball has shot to center right.
The Flying Scotman's rising! Watch that flight!
But Pullman Sleeper's chasing Demon Rum.
Here's Golden Rush—he's putting up a fight!
The dark horse of the race is stealing one!
I don't believe his luck! Young Perseus has won!"

37

"I told you so," the woman proudly crowed.
The man gave her an agitated glance.
She checked the odds to see what they were owed:
"I'll up the stakes and own this equine dance!"
"You're sure you want to risk another chance?"
"Are you a man? Do you not want the gold?"
The husband hung his head and looked askance:
"A woman ought to do what she is told."
Eliza put a finger to her lips, ice-cold.

38

"Was it so hard to leave their joy unspoiled?"
Eliza whirled her head 'round with a snap
and glared at Mr. Stone, her fingers coiled.
"They made their choice; they want to know the track."
"You fear their love and want its sweetness back."
"You'd keep her in a cage, without a life!"
"You'd keep him under her, a jumping jack."
She frowned and turned her gaze back on the wife
already digging in with stats to fuel the strife.

39

"My choice is Pegasus—he's sure to win!
And this one, Yacht Club Party, is for place.
But to score big we need to go all in.
For show, it's MoreLikeGuidelines in this race."
The husband shook his head and made a grimace.
"Percentages don't lie. Put Cetus first.
Or have your crystal vibes done a volte face?"
She scratched out Cetus from the list and cursed.
"My vision's clear. I choose, and then we win the purse."

40

The race man cried, "They gather for the storm!
Protect yourself; don't wind up in the red!"
The wife punched in her choices on the form;
her husband grit his teeth and shook his head.
"They're off! The field has breached the fountainhead!
I.O.U is jostling MoreLikeGuidelines.
Now Customs Carnet's broken Trusted Bonds,
while Underwriter's pushing for more time.
Lex Maritima has the herd in wake behind!"

41

The horse-wave pounded down the crashing straight,
a liquid mountain of electric flesh.
Their lungs were heaving with their flashing gait;
their hearts hurled rivers of their crimson stress.
The crowd of watchers roared its deep distress
as one by one the riders lost his nerve.
The roaring ghost of victory possessed
th'endragoned equines as they hit the curve.
White flecks of salt flew from their flanks—none dared to swerve.

42

"It's Pegasus come flying through the air,
but wait! Here's Bank Run on the inner track!
That flying horse is lost without a prayer!
No! Going Dutch is down...he's crossed his check!"
It happened in a flash, the herd ship-wrecked;
the lead horse foundered and fell to his knees.
A bell rang as the teller hit the deck
to signal that the bets were being seized.
The couple wailed their banishment and wept, aggrieved.

43

"You knew the stats? You threw that race for spite!"
The husband clenched his fists and snarled with rage.
"I made my choice—you want to pick a fight?!"
The wife turned cold and snapped, "You're not a sage!"
"I wanted Cetus, not that flying page!
Your garbage readings cost us our last coin!"
"At least I don't pretend it's the Bronze Age!"
She wheeled around and kicked him in the groin.
He buckled over, clutching his empurpling loins.

44

Unsatisfied, the wife grabbed for her glass;
a chuckle from Eliza set the mood.
"Some prize you are! You're such a sorry ass!"
Her husband yelled, "You classless little shrew!"
—and ducked to miss the glass and flying food.
His wife let loose another plate of snacks.
Her husband puffed his chest out for the feud:
"Look at that bitch who thinks she rules the nest!"
Eliza's giggles rose in sharp cascading jests.

45

"You're drunk, you bastard! Always with the snark!"
"At least I know when I've been pwned," he shot.
She took carafe in hand and crudely barked:
"Owned by a man who cannot shoot a shot!"
"Your mother should have murdered you, you thot!"
She smashed the glass and slashed out with a shard;
he lunged at her to stop the juggernaut.
The shard cut through to bone and past his guard;
he screamed and spat and made a fist to hit her hard.

46

He smashed his love with one throw of his fist
and cursed the evening for its deadly cost.
"You've ruined my face," his bride cried through the mist
of broken promises and futures lost;
"I curse the day we met—it was star-crossed!"
She took her ring of precious diamond stones
and threw it to the floor like cheap hoarfrost.
The dog sniffed at the gold to check for bones,
while in the ceiling doves flew round about their thrones.

47

The husband touched his face; the cuts dripped blood.
"Look what you made me do! How much we've lost!
I've no idea how we'll stem the flood
of debts and interest rates to cover costs."
He scrabbled for the ring that she had tossed
but cut his hands on hidden shards of glass.
He scoured the rubble like a geognost
oblivious to the screams of his lost lass.
Eliza tossed her head—and laughed and laughed and laughed.

48

A pair of hands pulled him from off the floor:
"It's time to crawl outside; you've had enough.
You take your wife; we'll head for that gold door—
you'll find your way is blocked to north and south."
"I'll not go anywhere without my stuff!"
The bouncer frowned and shook his head in grief:
"You kids had time to play—you played too rough."
"You and whose army?! You're a bloody thief!"
He marched them to the door; they cried in disbelief.

49

A drop of blood fell onto a white sheet
of paper marked with horses' names and kin.
"Why, Mr. Stone! You're wounded and effete!
But would you bleed to guarantee a win?"
He brushed his hand across his bloody skin—
a flying shard had cut into his cheek.
Eliza's faux concern changed to a grin.
"Some newlyweds, they couldn't last the week!
But they'll be back," she sniffed. "To chase that lucky streak."

50

The crash of dice and cards rose up the scale;
a one-armed bandit poured forth jingling coins.
"Jackpot!" a woman screeched and filled her pail
with lucky charms and joints of beef sirloin.
Her consort bent to roll another joint
while dealers rattled stacks of chips and hash.
High rollers swelled their pockets, bets conjoined;
a thousand points of light burned down to ash.
A sign flashed off and on and off: "Credit for cash!"

51

Above the din, amidst the flashing lights,
a slim white man stepped out upon the floor.
He wore a cape of satin, black as night,
and on his head, a hat of silk couture.
He trod the boards a dancer, self-assured.
His left hand twirled three shining crystal balls,
while with his right he tapped an overture
of power in a city without walls.
His gaze across the room held mirrors up to souls.

52

A single spotlight fell upon the stair
enticing him to mount up to the stage.
It shimmered in the light, not fully there
until a voice cried out, "Behold! the mage!"
A bow, a gesture towards a gilded cage;
the audience was eager for a show.
"Tonight is special," it intoned. "This sage
has journeyed far to make the dark night glow."
And with his cane he tapped, "A Hunting We Will Go."

53

The voice continued: "Lo! He comes to cast
a spell of making, past and present tense.
A story old as time, its futures vast.
The aether in his hands he can condense."
A smoky pall shot forth of pale incense;
the band began to play on brass and drums.
The rhythm rumored tales of wild suspense—
to hunt with hounds the auditorium
and know the fear of prey whose earthly end has come.

54

A flourish of his cape dispelled the smoke
that clung about his hands, now raised aloft
to summon ghostly minions and fair folk
and tempt the powers of heaven to his croft.
His voice was silk; his words and breath were soft:
"I sing the binding of the moon and sun,
the black and white, the heat and icy frost.
Who moves will not be moved by anyone,
yet he who sits like stone will sit not, but succumb."

55

He turned; his eye fell on the golden cage,
its single occupant a snow-white dove.
"Love is the mystery of our present age."
He paced around the cage, removed a glove.
"I call what is below from what's above
to form by will the form of your desire.
No power can wake the dead like that of love,
the force that chills like ice yet burns like fire."
With naked hand he reached inside the cage's wire.

56

The dove, head-bobbing, bowed her servitude
and stretched her wing-tips at her liberty.
Her talons clasped his finger, and she cooed;
she danced upon his hand in ecstasy.
"Observe the pigeon in her reverie!
What would you give to fly with her, and rest?"
He clasped her in one hand, cooed musically,
and calmed her flutt'ring nerves with a caress;
her heart beat strong beneath her gold and silver breast.

57

"What would you give to soar into the sky
and cross the heavens to the rising sun,
to spy horizons with an eagle eye
and find yourself in union with the One?
The dove knows where electric currents run
from pole to pole across the Milky Way
and where the dragon's courtiers pay the sum
to bind themselves until the Judgment Day
when King Osiris wakes from sleep their hearts to weigh."

58

A hush fell on the room; the people strained
to see the pigeon resting in his hand.
"What would you give to quest with her, unchained
from mortal coils of gravity and sand,
to drink with her the myrrh of Dragonland
and savor every merchant's hoarded spice?"
The men dreamed dreams of camel caravans;
the women dreamed of men they would entice
to lie with them for lust unpaid by wage of vice.

59

The charmer smiled and drew a cedar twig
across the feathers of the pigeon's breast.
"What would you give to see her die—but live?
Her heart beats now, but soon will be at rest."
He pressed the wand against her snow-white chest.
The thirsty crowd leaned in with bated breath;
the wizard whispered words of sweet caress
and drew from the dove's heart a silken thread,
a filament with which to bind a soul in death.

60

"The thread of life is spun by taking risks,
a roulette wheel of opportunity.
To grab a thread and pull it—that's the trick
to master death and life, earth, sky, and sea."
He tugged the silk and coiled it three times three,
then took a crystal glass out from his cloak.
The people sighed, entranced; the thread danced free
and dropped into the glass, becoming smoke.
"Now watch it whirl and curl, my coiling antidote!"

61

The vapor rose into the air and crawled
across the room in threads of emerald mist.
It roiled and coiled; the audience enthralled
forgot itself in pharmakeic bliss
while, still as stone, the dove sat on his wrist.
"I see a cloud!" "A snake!" "An open door!"—
the drunken people craved the dragon tryst.
"Breathe deeply of the mist; imbibe the lore!"—
the mage's hands cast magic out onto the floor.

62

A woman gasped, "I felt his hand touch me!"
Her womb convulsed with alchemic desire.
Another sobbed, "I'd die for his beauty."
A third made light, "I dare not risk the fire."
The swirling smoke rose from its ghostly pyre
to wreathe the room with columbine incense.
Its turning traced an ever-widening gyre
to wake the beast that feeds on innocence.
The men and women of the watching crowd grew tense.

63

The mage began to rap an ancient verse:
"The powers of the air are here tonight.
What one believes, must all or feel the curse.
A mystic transformation is your right:
breathe deep, and let the Dragon burn your fright.
Now, say with me: the circle can be squared,
the dove can best the falcon in a fight.
No fear can tame the lion with no fear;
the wolf lies with the lamb until the king appears."

64

His cane tapped on the floor, a metronome
to raise the dead and call the stars to kneel.
The pigeon smoke played round the pleasuredome
enticing men and women to reveal
their inmost yearning for Dame Fortune's wheel.
"The circle can be squared," the mage intoned.
"The corners of the earth a globe conceal.
What gravity can't move your will alone
can fix your diadem upon enchanted bone."

65

The crowd, aroused, began to rock and roll,
their movements synchronizing with the beat,
each tick and tock in tempo with the whole,
a whirling, twirling, tapping crash of feet.
The blood within began to rush with heat,
a distillation of the pigeon's heart,
a surge of force within them, once discrete,
now pulsing with the fire of ancient hearths
and flames that danced in caves where beasts were treasured arts.

66

"A new thing on the earth, the circle squared!"
The dancers joined in chanting with the mage.
"The dove of smoke must rise into the air!"
The people stretched their hands out towards the stage,
transformed into one creature by his gage.
"Let's square the circle, circle squared!" they pined.
"A circle squared to pay the love dove's wage!"
"The world will be yours, if you get in line!
It's sugar, spice, and all things nice—but first, you sign!"

67

The crowd, astounded, watched his tapping cane
move back and forth in tempo with their chant.
He lifted high the dove—they cried his name
and said he should have run for government.
"A mighty prince!" "A sage!" "An elephant!"
Their accolades resounded round the room.
"No one but you can ease our discontent!"
They offered made-up reasons for their gloom
and cried as if his alchemy could change their doom.

68

The sorcerer displayed the sleeping bird
and stroked her silent breast, no longer beating.
"She sleeps, but I can wake her with a word
and into life command her spirit streaming."
He whispered occult words with secret meaning.
Into her flesh his voice was then impressed;
he called her from the deepest realms of dreaming
and bound her with his will like one possessed,
the essence of his voice in wings made manifest.

69

"She lives!" a woman shrieked. "She wasn't dead,"
another chimed. A third began to sing.
"You breathed her life, and now she lives in death."
The mage's mesmerizing voice took wing
and soared above their heads, a splendid thing.
"Whom will she choose? Whose fortune will be made?"
All eyes turned to the lights that wheeled in rings
in promise of the riches to be paid.
The tapping of the mage's cane raised hearts to spades.

70

The dove flew o'er the crowd to find a perch
and hovered by the ceiling, gold and white.
Her feathers flashed in tempo as she searched
for someone upon whom she could alight,
a pillar of the realm to bear her plight.
A suited man stood tall and saturnine,
his face a picture of the passing night.
Upon his wrist a golden orb of time
turned seconds into hours that ate into his spine.

71

The man turned to his wife and gave a snort.
"It's smoke and mirrors! Entertaining lies!
He'd never pull it off without support.
Just let me up there, and I'll show you why
it only works if he is in disguise."
He flexed his hand as if to make a fist.
The pigeon cocked her head and took a dive,
her eye caught by the gold upon his wrist.
A peck, a turn—his watch was gone with a single twist.

72

"That pigeon stole my watch!" the tall man whined.
"Those filthy rats with wings, they're bloody thieves!"
"How dare that bird!" his wife, appalled, opined.
"That watch I gave you on our wedding eve!"
His face blanched as he searched the shadowed eaves,
recalling how they were engaged to wed.
The dove flew to the stage, watch in her beak;
the man clenched both his fists and wagged his head.
"I'll get it back," he snarled. "That dove's as good as dead."

73

The mage held out a hand for his beloved;
she flew to him, her purloined gift to give.
The dove alighted on his leather glove.
"What have we here?" he mused, contemplative.
"I see your game, you snake! That bird's a thief!"
The tall man stormed the stairs, two at a time.
"You want to tango?! I'll give you some grief!"
The mage received his guest with measured charm.
"Now, now, there's no one here who seeks to do you harm."

74

"Behold!" the mage smiled wide. "A volunteer!
Tell us about yourself, your secret dreams,
your hobbies and your broadcasting career!"
"You know my face, you must have seen my stream—
but you, I think, have come to town to scheme."
The mage bowed low, acknowledging the hit;
his tapping cane cut through the smoky beam.
"I come to test your wisdom and your wit.
In moments we will learn what you recall. Please, sit."

75

The tall man crossed the stage and took a seat.
The mage drew from his vest a silver chain
and from the dove he took the golden treat.
"This watch you wear—a symbol of your reign?"
"It keeps the time, if that is what you mean."
The mage secured the chain to the gold band.
"Let's see what secrets lie in your domain."
He swung the watch, now dangling from his hand.
The tall man's gaze grew dim as time turned into sand.

76

"Your eyes are getting heavy; you may sleep!
Be easy now; take rest. Try not to blink.
Recall that font that flows within the deep
of every dream of elephants, bright pink.
In Nubia, where wheels turn at the brink
of stories bound with magic to enchant.
Flamingoes from the furthest sulphur drink
the mysteries of the burning saline sands.
The rhythms of their feet volcanic beat expands."

77

The tall man sighed and sank into a dream.
His eye now focused on the fountain scene,
he rode the resonance in his bloodstream.
The watch swung back and forth against the screen
of smoke and lights and memories unseen.
The mage's voice beguiled him into sleep;
his mind set sail along the riverine
and plunged his heart into the dungeon keep
where monsters lurk, and serpents writhe, and dragons creep.

78

"Tell us your name," the mage's voice intoned;
"a noble man should know his lineage."
"My father was a Stern," the tall man groaned;
"he called me Churchill, child of his old age.
He hoped it would recall my parentage."
"An orphan," breathed the mage. "We are in luck!
No father's whim can claim your maritage,
as rings you run around this faceless ruck."
The tall man gave a jolt as if he had been struck.

79

"Be easy now, and tell us what you spy."
"I see the stars and planets in their dome
and four stone pillars reaching to the sky.
I see a basin bronze of oxen chrome
with people standing 'round it soon to die.
I see a pavement carved with monstrous beasts;
a dragon spits down water from on high.
I see a court of princes at a feast
inhaling spices brought by merchants from the East."

80

The mage looked pleased. "You have an eye for signs—
but can you parse their sense, unlock their wyrd?"
The tall man stared, eyes closed, at the designs.
"I see a kind of pattern in the sphere—
it's set there to deceive, but I see clear.
The pillars are a trick to hold the dome,
raised up by a celestial engineer.
The oxen hold the waters of our home
established with creation's first exploding ohm."

81

"That's it?" the mage looked at his fingernails.
"Your vision's sound, but not a big surprise.
A child could tell as much from nursery tales.
You'll have to use a better glass to scry."
"I'm sure your other fans are mystified,
but I know how to see through all the spells.
The pavement beasts are symbols of your lies;
those princes getting high are priests of hell
collecting coins that fools throw in that wishing well."

82

"Your mind—it wheels around without reprieve.
Perhaps a game to take away the dread;
a game of chance should help you to believe
that I alone can resurrect the dead.
Your intellect might question this new thread;
no need to reason, you can simply feel.
One simple spin—we'll see what's in your head.
A Churchill ought to know the patterned wheel
with which the old make new the turnings of the real."

83

The mage turned to the audience and clapped:
"Who wants to try his hand at beating Fate?"
He pressed his fingers tight; the tension snapped.
"A fortune's to be won—by one or eight.
I have the tickets here to validate
a company of seven for the quest.
Hands up! Be quick! You don't want to be late!
Wonders demand that Time itself is pressed.
Who wants to fly without the beating in their chest?"

84

He set the dove to wheel above their hands
outstretched into the aether of the deep.
She soared on currents crossed by silver bands
of smoke that lulled the audience to sleep.
On verge of tears, they fought the urge to weep,
as down into their dreams the pigeon dove
to wrest from hearts a secret they would keep
to win from dragon's hoard a treasure trove
and chart a starry map to end their restless rove.

85

"I want to play!" a gold-haired woman wooed;
she pursed her lips and twirled her fuscia gown.
The dove descending on her, circling flew;
a diamond circlet graced the woman's brow.
"Our first contender! Don't be shy! Come down!"
the mage undressed her with an icy glance.
She blinked and smiled. "A night out on the town!"
The men leered at her as she seized her chance
to dance and win jewelled pledges of her heart's romance.

86

Another man erupted onto stage.
"Let's make a deal! I've gotta know your tricks!"
He gestured towards the dove above the mage.
"They're golden wheels inside that make it tick?
I'll offer you six figures for the shtick."
He pushed his way upstage and gave a grin.
"I've run a show like this—it's politics!
The main thing is, you have to play to win.
Just let me have that dove, and we'll be in like Flynn!"

87

A third rose up, a man in sable mink.
"I'm in to win that bird, I need to fly!"
He rushed the stage. "I'll tell you what I think!"
—and with the mage he locked him eye-to-eye.
"It is full proof, the fools know truth tests lies."
He pointed to the dove, chanting in tone:
"She swoops to scoop up all our alibis;
our secret iconology she'll comb,
the dark desires and fantasies below our bone."

88

A spotlight swept the room, paused here and there,
then lit upon a flowing satin gown.
Demurely the young woman tossed her hair
and glanced at all the people standing round.
"A princess!" someone gasped. She made no sound
but turned from side to side to catch the light.
"You'll do," the mage said, "if you're virgin found."
She turned away, but moved still in his sight,
while longing for the sovereignty to rule the night.

89

"We've conquered the whole earth, why not the moon?"
A man without a hat inquired at large.
"A mere ten years, and it will be high noon.
We can't slow down—it's upwards we must charge!"
"You have ambition," crowed the mage. "Yes, Sarge!
I seek to join the ranks of manly men."
"You've won your place on the contestants' barge.
Come join the others on the podium."
The hatless man assumed the stage, eager to win.

90

Then suddenly beyond the mage's frame
a quiet Stone called out to self-conscript.
"I'll take the final place within the Game."
"A ringer!" the mage laughed. "You'll sink the ship!"
The Harlequin moved towards the stage, and quipped:
"A penny earned's a penny saved from debt.
And magic rhymes bear secrets from Egypt!"
The mage looked dazzled for a beat, then rapped:
"The Company is formed; it's time to place your bets!"

91

The audience erupted with a roar
and shook their fists now crisp with betting slips.
The spotlight panned across the heaving floor
and paused on each contestant for a blip.
They jostled for position on the ship,
upstaging one another to be seen,
and clutched their tickets, longing for the trip.
"The game begins! Who will be king or queen?!"
The mage recalled the pigeon from her soaring dream.

92

The mage turned round, a finger to his lips;
his gaze was subtly Mephistophelean.
"Who'll be the first to brave apocalypse
and join the ranks of starry champions?"
The spotlight raked the stage, then zeroed in
upon a curtain circling the room.
Its colors wrung from shellfish Tyrian,
its patterns spoke of mystics, sigils, doom.
No woman's hand had cast the shuttle on its loom.

93

The fabric shimmered in the coursing light.
The pigeon took her rest, no heart to feel.
The mage looked left, glanced up, glared down, looked right.
The curtain opened to reveal a Wheel
engraved with letters of a battle shield.
Its hub was crystal from the firmament;
its spokes were seven, set with bright beryl.
Upon its cycles hung the government
of planetary myst'ries, hearts, and joys for rent.

94

"Your trip awaits," the mage intoned, "a quest
to square the circle hidden in the Wheel.
One spin, and you will ride the breaking crest
of secrets hoarded in the ancient weal."
He urged them to approach the magic seal.
"I know that song," the man in mink exclaimed.
"It calls to me in dreams, 'Khemet, you real!'"
He started humming rhythms, entertained.
"This fantasy, it haunts my thoughts; the dark enflamed."

95

"Come, spin the Wheel, and open the star realm."
The mage's voice was low and resonant.
The man in mink stepped up to seize the helm
and caught his image in the beryl's glint.
He grasped the Wheel and pressed his fingerprint
upon its shining edges as he spun.
The cold crystal within sparked beguilement.
His eyes were drawn inside it as it shone.
The gyre of lights absorbed him, and the two were one.

96

The watchers blinked; the man was gone! But, no—
"I see him in the screen above the stage!"
His image gave a bow to those below,
 a giant of the electronic age.
The others lined up quick behind the mage,
each eager to step up and be transformed.
"Just say your name and with the Wheel engage,
and you will join the court of the informed—
where you will breathe the spice and be by aether formed."

97

The hatless man stepped forward, head held high.
"My name is Maro on my father's side."
He touched the Wheel and vanished in the sky.
"Oh, I'm with him," the gold-haired woman sighed.
She sang a little song: "I'm Lorelei."
"You stick with me," the dealer took her arm.
"I'm Dominic; come with me for the ride."
She blushed, "Why sure, I'll be your lucky charm!"
And through the Wheel they stepped to taste electric balm.

98

The mage addressed the next in line: "Your turn."
Her face in profile could have been a coin:
"I fear the turning of the Wheel—it burns."
"You fear a trick?" asked Stone. "Your trust purloined?"
"I know the way," said Stern. "It's happy loins."
The virgin turned to Stone, her face in full,
to say her name and enter the Wheel's joys:
"I'm Helen of the ancient family Coel.
I know that when you touch the Wheel, you wage your soul."

99

She touched the Wheel and faded into time.
"I'm Stern," the fourth man said and followed suit.
"You're last," the mage told Damian in rhyme.
He took a bow and said, "I know the route."
The Wheel revolved, and Stone felt it transmute
incarnate bodies into ghosts sublimed.
Their figures in the glass seemed to permute,
seen darkly in the stellar pantomime.
The audience erupted, shouting out in time:

100

"Let's square the circle! Circles must be squared!"
The Wheel hummed with celestial energy.
The stars began to dance in Aion's lair;
their oscillating sparks fueled synergy.
The mage held out his hands in sign of three
and clapped to bring the Wheel to rest once more.
The prism slowed its spin in short degrees.
Its colors flashed and merged to close the door,
but ere it shut, a dog leapt through the cyclic core.

To be continued…

With planets in his eyes, he turned his head
and sang to her of Empires filled with joy and dread:

"Come near, my dove, and taste the hidden love.
Into a dream I'll ease you, ne'er to wake.
One tear to taste, like star-milk from above,
shows lights unseen unless you dare partake.
Sharp on your tongue, a pyramid of snakes
uncloaks a dark star burning in my breast.
You'll see the world as clearly as the drakes,
and capture seas from East to furthest West.
For Dragon sight, I'll trade the crystal in your chest."

About the Editor

Rachel Fulton Brown is Associate Professor of History at the University of Chicago, where she teaches courses on the history of Christianity, medieval European religious, cultural, and intellectual history, and the works of J.R.R. Tolkien. She is the author of *From Judgment to Passion: Devotion to Christ and the Virgin Mary, 800-1200* (2002), and *Mary and the Art of Prayer: The Hours of the Virgin in Medieval Christian Life and Thought* (2017), and she has held fellowships from the Guggenheim Foundation, the Mellon Foundation, the American Council of Learned Societies, and the National Humanities Center, among others. In her public life, she blogs as *Fencing Bear at Prayer*, and she lectures on Logos, Tolkien, and medieval history at Unauthorized.tv. The Dragon Common Room is her online forum for training poets in the arts of the Christian imagination. She livestreams weekly on *The Mosaic Ark*, where she and co-host Kilts Khalfan will take you on a mystical journey through the history, mythology, and symbolism of the Internet.

Acknowledgments

We are grateful to everyone who so generously supported our Kickstarter, both named and unnamed.

Alejandro López Baragaño
Anthony Baratta
Joseph D. Barnes, Jr.
V. A. Boston
Christopher Jacob Carter
Travis J. I. Corcoran
Gabriel E
Danielle Gaines
Samuel Hardie
Jordan A. Johnson
Alexander Kubinski
Nicholas James McGouran
David McIver
James Nealon
Cole Pero
SirHamster
Conway Q. Tomlinson

We thank especially those who have backed our efforts for all five Acts, and we look forward to sharing Damian's journey with you as he goes to Hell—and back. Here be dragons... and doves.

* 9 7 9 8 2 1 8 2 5 6 9 6 8 *